D1304287

*T*he nicest thing about the future
is that it comes one day at a time.

Anonymous

Other books in the *"Language of" Series...*

Blue Mountain Arts®

The Language of Courage and Inner Strength

The Language of Friendship

The Language of Happiness

The Language of Love

The Language of Marriage

The Language of Positive Thinking

The Language of Prayer

The Language of Success

The Language of Teaching

The Language of Teenagers

Thoughts to Share with a Wonderful Mother

Thoughts to Share with a Wonderful Father

Thoughts to Share with a Wonderful Son

Thoughts to Share with a Wonderful Daughter

It's Great to Have a Brother like You

It's Great to Have a Sister like You

➤

The Language of

RECOVERY

A Blue Mountain Arts® Collection

SPS Studios, Inc., Boulder, Colorado

Library of Congress Catalog Card Number: 00-035242
ISBN: 1-58786-001-5

ACKNOWLEDGMENTS appear on page 48.

Certain trademarks are used under license.

Manufactured in Thailand
First Printing: April 2000

 This book is printed on recycled paper.

Library of Congress Cataloging-in-Publication Data

The language of recovery : a Blue Mountain Arts collection.
    p.   cm.
  ISBN 1-58786-001-5
  1. Conduct of life--Quotations, maxims, etc. 2. Conduct of life--Poetry.
I. SPS Studios.

PN6084.C556 L36   2000
082--dc21   00-035242

SPS Studios, Inc.

P.O. Box 4549, Boulder, Colorado 80306

Contents

(Authors listed in order of first appearance)

Vicki Silvers
R. L. Keith
Karen Berry
Hippocrates
A Course in Miracles
Oliver Wendell Holmes
Donna Newman
Deanna Beisser
Regina Hill
Deepak Chopra
Melody Beattie
Robert Louis Stevenson
Veronica A. Shoffstall
Bernie S. Siegel, M.D.
Dale Carnegie
Dag Hammarskjöld
Donna Fargo
Matthew Arnold
Susan L. Taylor
Jules Jusserand
Syrus
Ellen Browning Scripps
Shakti Gawain
Lao-Tse
Chinese Proverb
Susan Polis Schutz

Victor Hugo
William A. McGarey, M.D.
Henry Ward Beecher
Carl G. Jung
St. Francis of Assisi
Andrew Harding Allen
Louise L. Hay
Joseph D. Beasley
   and Susan Knightly
Julia Cameron
Leo Tolstoy
James Allen
Napoleon Bonaparte
Josie Willis
Collin McCarty
Douglas Pagels
Linda E. Knight
Alin Austin
Anna Marie Edwards
Joan Borysenko
Rachel Naomi Remen
Douglas Richards
Gerald Jampolsky
Tim Connor
Wendy Apgar
Molière

Alexander Pope
Samuel Smiles
Old English Legend
Joseph Campbell
Albert Camus
Maurice Maeterlinck
Marcus Aurelius
Joan and Miroslav Borysenko
Barbara J. Hall
Orison Swett Marden
Emily Dickinson
James L. Allen
Virgil
A. J. Cronin
Henry Wadsworth Longfellow
Hugh Prather
Leigh Mitchell Hodges
Barbara Cage
Emmet Fox
Jim McGregor
Sir Joshua Reynolds
Caroline Myss
Reinhold Niebuhr
Julia Escobar
Polar Eskimo Saying
Acknowledgments

Walk Your Path One Step at a Time

Life's circumstances are not always what you might wish them to be. The pattern of life does not necessarily go as you plan. Beyond any understanding, you may at times be led in different directions that you never imagined, dreamed, or designed. Yet if you had never put any effort into choosing a path, or tried to carry out your dream, then perhaps you would have no direction at all.

Rather than wondering about or questioning the direction your life has taken, accept the fact that there is a path before you now. Shake off the "why's" and "what if's," and rid yourself of confusion. Whatever was — is in the past. Whatever is — is what's important. The past is a brief reflection. The future is yet to be realized. Today is here.

Walk your path one step at a time — with courage, faith, and determination. Keep your head up, and cast your dreams to the stars. Soon your steps will become firm and your footing will be solid again. A path that you never imagined will become the most comfortable direction you could have ever hoped to follow.

Keep your belief in yourself and walk into your new journey. You will find it magnificent, spectacular, and beyond your wildest imaginings.

— Vicki Silvers

As you begin your journey, know that in the grand scheme of things, we live in a world where rainy days eventually give way to sunnier skies, and where simply believing in tomorrow takes you halfway up the mountain to getting beyond any difficulties.

May you have the companionship of comfort on every path you take and the gentleness of peace. May you find serenity and strength and every single thing... that will put your heart at ease.

— R. L. Keith

We cannot change the past;
we just need to keep the good memories
and acquire wisdom
from the mistakes we've made.
We cannot predict the future;
we just need to hope and pray
for the best and what is right,
and believe that's how it will be.
We can live a day at a time,
enjoying the present
and always seeking to become
a more loving and better person.

 Karen Berry

The natural healing force within each one of us is the greatest force in getting well.

Hippocrates

Every situation, properly perceived, becomes an opportunity to heal.

A Course in Miracles

The great thing
in this world
is not so much
where we are,
but in what direction
we are moving.

Oliver Wendell Holmes

What Is Recovery?

Rebuilding our lives,
Restoring ourselves,
Picking up the pieces,
Healing from past wounds,
Regaining our hope,
Obtaining self-respect,
Mending broken spirits,
Making amends for the spirits we've broken,
Reclaiming our right to be,
Releasing what doesn't belong to us,
Raising up what does without fear,
Repossessing our minds and our hearts,
Repairing broken thoughts and faulty behaviors,
Replacing them with thoughts and acts of love,
Renewing our faith, our minds, and our bodies,
Reviving life within and around us,
Realizing that there is good within us,
Growing in our ability to feel and express that good,
Renovating our broken dreams and broken hearts,
Increasing our ability to own our light,
Reaching out to lovingly share that light with others.

Donna Newman

There may be days when you get up in the morning
and things aren't the way you had hoped they would be.
That's when you have to tell yourself that things will get better.
There are times when people disappoint you and let you down,
but those are the times when you must remind yourself
to trust your own judgments and opinions,
to keep your life focused on believing in yourself
    and all that you are capable of.

There will be challenges to face and changes to make in your life,
and it is up to you to accept them.
Constantly keep yourself headed in the right direction for you.
It may not be easy at times, but in those times of struggle
you will find a stronger sense of who you are,
and you will also see yourself developing
into the person you have always wanted to be.

Life is a journey through time, filled with many choices;
each of us will experience life in our own special way.
So when the days come that are filled
with frustration and unexpected responsibilities,
remember to believe in yourself and all you want your life to be,
because the challenges and changes will only help you to find
the dreams that you know are meant to come true for you.

 — Deanna Beisser

Acceptance

Acceptance means that you can find the serenity within
to let go of the past with its mistakes and regrets,
move into the future with a new perspective,
and appreciate the opportunity to take a second chance.

Acceptance means that when difficult times come into your life,
you'll find security again and comfort to relieve any pain.
You'll find new dreams, fresh hopes, and forgiveness of the heart.

Acceptance does not mean that you will always be perfect.
It simply means that you'll always overcome imperfection.

Acceptance is the road to peace — letting go of the worst,
holding on to the best, and finding the hope inside
that continues throughout life.

Acceptance is the heart's best defense,
love's greatest asset, and the easiest way
    to keep believing in yourself and others.

— Regina Hill

Accept what comes to you
totally and completely so that you
can appreciate it, learn from it, and
then let it go.

Deepak Chopra

Sometimes when we pray for miracles, what
we're really praying for is help in skipping steps,
for shortcuts. The simple act of acceptance, of
returning to each step of our path, can often
bring us the miracle we need. Then we see the
truth. The real miracle is one always available to
each of us: it's the miracle of acceptance. We can
go where we want to go, one step at a time.

Melody Beattie

Anyone can carry his burden, however hard, until nightfall.
Anyone can do his work, however hard, for one day.

Robert Louis Stevenson

After a While

After a while you learn
the subtle difference between holding a hand and chaining a soul
and you learn
that love doesn't mean leaning
and company doesn't always mean security.
And you begin to learn
that kisses aren't contracts and presents aren't promises
and you begin to accept your defeats with your head up and your eyes ahead
with the grace of a woman, not the grief of a child
and you learn
to build all your roads on today because tomorrow's ground is
too uncertain for plans
and futures have a way of falling down in mid-flight.
After a while you learn
that even sunshine burns if you get too much
so you plant your own garden and decorate your own soul
instead of waiting for someone to bring you flowers.
And you learn that you really can endure
you really are strong
you really do have worth
and you learn
and you learn
with every goodbye, you learn...

Veronica A. Shoffstall

Life is difficult. Think of breaking up the difficulties into small pieces, small steps. And share the difficulties — then they may become bearable. The secret is learning to live with and to use the difficulties one encounters.

 Bernie S. Siegel, M.D.

Remember how a walking trip always seems shorter if we concentrate, not on the total distance to our destination, but just the distance to the next milepost. In the same way, we should concentrate on living within today. Then better tomorrows will inevitably follow.

Dale Carnegie

Never look down to test the ground before taking your next step: only he who keeps his eye fixed on the far horizon will find his right road.

Dag Hammarskjöld

You'll Get Through This...
One Day at a Time

Try not to worry. Try to look at what you're going through as a challenge rather than an obstacle, a time to develop patience. To achieve more objectivity, detach yourself from the struggle. Have confidence in yourself, and realize that you can change your attitude even if you can't change the circumstances.

Look closely at your troubles. Don't let them cause you to give up. Befriend them and learn from them. Feel them lose their power over you. Allow them to teach you what you want to know and move on. Try not to be afraid.

You're a survivor. You're going to handle this. You're going to find strength you didn't know you had and grace to deal with whatever comes along. Pretty soon, you'll be on the other side, and it's just a matter of time until you will look back on this time in your life and draw strength from the knowledge that even though the road was rocky, you persevered and carried on.

— Donna Fargo

Resolve to be thyself: and know, that he who finds himself, loses his misery.

— Matthew Arnold

We bring about new beginnings by deciding to bring about endings. To renew your life you must be willing to change, to make an effort to leave behind the things that compromise your wholeness. The universe rushes to support you whenever you attempt to take a step forward. Any time you seek to be in harmony with life, to make yourself feel more whole, all the blessings that flow from God stream toward you, to bolster you and encourage you, because all life is biased on the side of supporting itself.

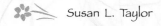   Susan L. Taylor

Remember this, and also be persuaded of its truth —
the future is not in the hands of fate, but in ourselves.

   Jules Jusserand

It matters not what you are thought to be,
but what you are.

                    Syrus

Every day is a birthday, for every day we are born anew.

                    Ellen Browning Scripps

An essential part of the process of healing has to do with going into the shadow aspects of ourselves — the aspects that, out of fear, we have denied, disowned, or suppressed. Beginning in a gradual, safe, and comfortable way, we can accept and include them. Then, by allowing them their natural expression, we start to become more fully integrated human beings.

Shakti Gawain

The tree which needs two arms to span its girth sprang from the tiniest shoot. Yon tower, nine stories high, rose from a little mound of earth. A journey of a thousand miles began with a single step.

Lao-Tse

The man who removes a mountain begins by carrying away small stones.

Chinese Proverb

Many people
go from one thing
to another
searching for happiness
But with each new venture
they find themselves
more confused
and less happy
until they discover
that what they are
searching for
is inside themselves
and what will make them happy
is sharing their real selves
with the ones they love

 — Susan Polis Schutz

Above the cloud
    with its shadow
Is the star
    with its light.

 Victor Hugo

Put knowledge, faith, and ideals into action...

Create an ideal for your life that you are willing to follow. Let it be something that is creative and constructive, never destructive or for the self alone. Identify for yourself what higher force you really believe in. Then act as if you have faith in that higher force that you will be guided and shown the way through your life, as well as through your search for healing. In other words, act as if these things are real in your life, and then *take action*.

> William A. McGarey, M.D.

The little troubles and worries of life, so many of which we meet, may be as stumbling blocks in our way, or we may make them steppingstones to a noble character and to Heaven.

Troubles are often the tools by which God fashions us for better things.

> Henry Ward Beecher

A whole person is one who has both walked with God and wrestled with the devil.

> Carl G. Jung

Lord, make me an instrument
of your peace.
Where there is hatred,
let me sow love;
where there is injury, pardon;
where there is doubt, faith;
where there is despair, hope;
where there is darkness, light;
and where there is sadness, joy.

 St. Francis of Assisi

God grant me the strength
to reach out for my dreams
and see the world
with understanding and love,
and to believe in the beauty
of life and the dignity of mankind.

 Andrew Harding Allen

We create our reality with our minds. If we want to change our reality, then it's time for us to change our minds. We do this by choosing to think and speak in new and positive ways. I learned a long time ago that if I would change my thinking, I could change my life. Changing our thinking is really dropping our limitations. As we drop our limitations, we begin to be aware of the infinity of life all around us. We begin to understand that we are already perfect, whole, and complete. Each day gets easier.

 — Louise. L. Hay

Recovery from any illness involves the body, the mind, and the spirit. Together, these three elements make up who we are, and true healing includes all these aspects of the self. Like a three-legged stool, recovery cannot stay upright and balanced unless all three "legs" are equally strong.

Joseph D. Beasley and Susan Knightly

In every event, in every circumstance, we have a choice of perspective. Faced with difficulty, we can choose between disappointment and curiosity as our mind-set. The choice is ours. Will we focus on what we see as lacking or will we look for the new good that is emerging? In every moment, however perilous or sorrowful it may feel, there is the seed of our greater happiness, greater expansion, and greater abundance.

Julia Cameron

Now is the only time over which we have dominion.

Leo Tolstoy

What you are, so is your world.

James Allen

The only conquests which are permanent and leave no regrets, are our conquests over ourselves.

Napoleon Bonaparte

Recovery Is...

...about learning that you have a choice: You can choose to be hopeful rather than hopeless; you can choose to act from faith rather than react from fear; and you can choose to enjoy life rather than merely survive it.

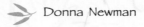 Donna Newman

...sometimes a long road. But take heart and keep the faith. Know that at the end of the dark tunnel there is a light. The answer lies within you, in the spirit with which you brave the battle. The pain and suffering are not you, but only a part of you.

 Josie Willis

...getting rid of the "if only's" and getting on with whatever you need to do to get things right.

 Collin McCarty

...realizing that what seems like a big deal today may be more manageable tomorrow...

Understand that time is on your side! You don't just have the next twenty-four hours to make things right. The truth is... you've got all the rest of your life.

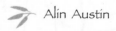 Douglas Pagels

...replacing your weaknesses with positives;
taking life's broken pieces and re-creating your dreams;
never measuring the future by the past;
letting yesterday become a memory
and tomorrow a promise.

Linda E. Knight

...realizing that the fullness of life awaits you, and that the difficult struggle will turn into the divine path.

Alin Austin

...a period of growth, self-discovery, and healing.

 Anna Marie Edwards

Healing Is...

...peeling away the barriers of fear that keep us unaware of our true nature of love, peace, and rich interconnection with the web of life. Healing is the rediscovery of who we are and who we have always been.

— Joan Borysenko

...natural. It's not magical; it's not mystical. It doesn't require some esoteric intervention. It's your birthright, and mine. Everybody has the capacity for healing. We do it with each other all the time and we don't even know it.

Healing is the very ground of being. Everything is moving toward wholeness. And that's all healing is, that movement. Our task is not to make something happen but to uncover what is already happening in us and in others, and to recognize and foster those conditions that nurture it. That's all.

We can do that with ritual or prayer, or with many different approaches and techniques. We can simply sit and be together and think about our true nature. No one technique is inherently any better than another. It's simply a matter of learning to trust the natural healing process in all of us and moving freely with it.

— Rachel Naomi Remen

...knowing when to work your mind and let your body relax, and when doing just the opposite makes the most sense.

 Douglas Richards

...releasing from the past. It is retraining my mind so as not to see the shadow of the past on anyone. It is learning not to make interpretations of people's behavior or motives. It is letting go of the desire to want to change another person. It is letting go of expectations, assumptions, and the desire to control or manipulate another person....

Healing is knowing that forgiveness is the key to happiness and offers me everything that I want. Healing is knowing that the only reality in the universe is love, and that love is the most important healer known to the world.

To heal is to trust in a creative force that is loving and forgiving, and to know in our hearts that there is no separation and we are all joined in love with God and each other. It means that all hearts and minds are joined as one....

Healing is letting go of the fearful child so many of us carry inside, and awakening to the innocent child who has always been within us.

 Gerald Jampolsky

My Wounded Child

Years ago the child in me was wounded by the world, well meaning
as it was.

The scars of yesterday remain etched on my being,
taking their toll on all my days and nights.
Looking back I can see the errors of those around me. Little did
they know the pain and suffering they would bring me.
Now that I am older I search for that loving open child that was.
But he remains in hiding from the pain that today might bring.
I want to set him free, so that my life can be anew. But to reach him
I must look deep into the pain and the past. He protects himself with
games that he plays. Games of guilt and anger and fear and resentment.
There is no winner in these games. For me to be free he must be
free to act and react not as the world expects but as he feels is right.

Those around may not understand the turmoil and grief I feel for
his suffering. I'm not even sure who he is anymore but I know
when he comes forth that I will love him.

For he is the me I used to be and want to be again.
The me that is real.
I have missed him all these years and it is time for him to have
his say. To guide my feelings and my growth. It is time for him
to set my world right. He has been gone too long.

I welcome him now to brighten my future and change my ways.
To help me laugh and love again in ways only he knows how.

For when he returns, you may not know me. But that's ok,
for he will love you just the same. He will bring a smile to your
face and love to your heart.

 Tim Connor

Life

I feel I'm on a roller coaster,
Especially these past few weeks.
One day I'm up, the next I'm down,
When balance is what I seek.

On one day I deal with the present,
Or the past I'm working through;
And then come my fears for the future,
Uncertainties old and new....

But also mixed in with the hard times
Are the small moments of joy.
Times I am blessed with hope and with peace
And friends whom I enjoy.

Life is comprised of both good and bad
No matter what I go through.
Moments of laughter and joy and love,
Mixed with the old and the new.

 Wendy Apgar

E very mountain means at least two valleys.

Anonymous

Do Not Be Afraid...

The greater the obstacle the more glory in overcoming it.

> Molière

A man should never be ashamed to say he has been in the wrong, which is but saying in other words that he is wiser today than he was yesterday.

> Alexander Pope

Probably he who never made a mistake never made a discovery.

> Samuel Smiles

Fear knocked at the door. Faith answered. No one was there.

> Old English Legend

It is only by going down into the abyss
that we recover the treasures of life.
Where you stumble,
there lies your treasure.
The very cave you are afraid to enter
turns out to be the source of
what you were looking for.

> Joseph Campbell

In the midst of
winter, I finally
learned that there
was in me an
invincible summer.

 Albert Camus

Find places of healing. Discover people, things, and places that nourish your soul, bring you back to center, help you heal.

Life is not an endurance contest. Not anymore. We are not in a race to see how long we can go without, how much we can go without, how much pain we can stay in. Although sometimes we go through dry spells and droughts, we are not cactuses.

There is a place in each of us that wants to heal, that can heal, that will heal. It's a peaceful place, one of nourishment, replenishment, peace, safety, comfort, and joy. It's a place of love and acceptance. It's a place of forgiveness, honesty, openness, nurturing, and kindness. You can find it quickly, if that's what you're seeking. You will recognize it instantly because of how it feels. It will bring you back to center. It will bring you back to calm. It will bring you back to joy.

— Melody Beattie

Let your task be to render yourself worthy of love and this even more for your own happiness than for that of another.

Maurice Maeterlinck

It is in your power to withdraw into yourself whenever you desire. Perfect tranquility within consists in the good ordering of the mind, — the realm of your own.

Marcus Aurelius

If you seek peace and love first, if you learn to become mindfully present, you'll find that good things seem to be attracted to you without your even having to specify them. When you think about using the power of your mind in daily life, remember that peace is the most important goal, because thoughts of peace open the heart to love, and they close the mind to fear. Peace and love are the frame of reference through which we discover the mind's true power.

Joan and Miroslav Borysenko

Nothing wastes more energy than worrying.
The longer one carries a problem, the heavier it gets.
Don't take things too seriously.
Live a life of serenity, not a life of regrets.

Douglas Pagels

Trust the Process of Life

If something happens that you feel you have no control over, then affirm a positive statement immediately. Keep saying it over and over to yourself until you move through that little space. When things don't feel right, you might say this to yourself: "All is well, all is well, all is well." Whenever you feel the urge to control things, you could say, "I trust the process of life."... In this way, whatever happens is okay because you are in harmony with the flow of life.

 — Louise L. Hay

Remember: the will is mighty. The steadfast decision and concerted effort to get better will begin to empower you. Hold fast to your desires and positive affirmation for wholeness and believe that you will recover completely. Don't be afraid to ask God for help, and it's important to thank Him and trust in Him that your prayers will be answered. He delights in our trust and praise and faithfulness.

— Donna Fargo

Survivors Always Find a Way
to Make the Best of Life

Survivors are people who have faced adversity
and won. They've had all the odds against them,
yet they've found a way to reach their goals.

Survivors are people who have been hurt by
circumstances, by others, or just by being in the
wrong place at the wrong time — but they don't
allow themselves to live in pain forever. They go
on, because they're brave enough and strong
enough to overcome. They face the future with
purpose, for they believe that time is on their
side and each effort will pay off.

Survivors know how to make the best of life.
They have an optimistic attitude and a winning
spirit. That's how they reach their goals, and
why success is now the story of their lives.

 Barbara J. Hall

With Hope and Courage,
You Will Triumph

There is no medicine like hope, no incentive so great, and no tonic so powerful as expectation of something better tomorrow.

— Orison Swett Marden

Hope is the thing with feathers
That perches in the soul,
And sings the tune without the words,
And never stops at all.

— Emily Dickinson

Be like the bird
That, pausing in her flight
Awhile on boughs too slight,
   Feels them give way
Beneath her and yet sings,
Knowing that she hath wings.

 Victor Hugo

Whether you be man or woman
you will never do anything in this
world without courage. It is the
greatest quality of the mind next
to honor.
> James L. Allen

They can conquer who believe they can.

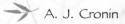 Virgil

Worry never robs tomorrow of its sorrow;
it only saps today of its strength.

> A. J. Cronin

Our todays and yesterdays are the blocks
with which we build.

 Henry Wadsworth Longfellow

Letting Go...

To have a hold on us... misery must be mentally reentered daily, and the doorway we provide is our preoccupation with what happened. There is very little that can hurt you once you learn how to release your mind from what you have unconsciously picked up during the day.

Hugh Prather

However you have used gone days, you can start afresh each morning, if you so desire. You can use this day for consolidating past gains of spirit, brain and hand, or you can use it for tearing down the old structure of self and laying the foundations for a new building. Each night of life is a wall between today and the past. Each morning is the open door to a new world — new vistas, new aims, new tryings....

However discouraging your days may have been thus far, keep this thought burning brightly in your mind — Life Begins Each Morning!

Leigh Mitchell Hodges

When things are not going right
don't give up — just try harder
Give yourself freedom to try out new things
Laugh and have a good time
Open yourself up to love
Take part in the beauty of nature
Be appreciative of all that you have
Help those less fortunate than you
Work towards peace in the world
Live life to the fullest
Create your own dreams and
follow them until they are a reality

 Susan Polis Schutz

If you can forgive yourself as well as others and learn from your mistakes, problems and heartaches will be steppingstones on your path to growing wiser and stronger.

If you can love yourself as well as others, you will learn acceptance and understanding.

If you believe you are unique and wonderful, then you will learn to change what you can, make a difference when you can, and accept the things you can't do anything about.

Barbara Cage

When someone you love has difficulties, listen.
When you're feeling terrible that you can't provide a
cure, listen. When you don't know what to offer the
people you care about, listen, listen, listen.

— Bernie S. Siegel, M.D.

The use of love is to heal.
When it flows without effort
from the depth of the self,
love creates health.

— Deepak Chopra

Love

There is no difficulty that enough love will not conquer;
No disease that enough love will not heal; No door that
enough love will not open; No gulf that enough love will
not bridge; No wall that enough love will not throw down;
No sin that enough love will not redeem...

It makes no difference how deeply seated may be the
trouble; How hopeless the outlook; How muddled the
tangle; How great the mistake. A sufficient realization of
love will dissolve it all... If only you could love enough
you would be the happiest and most powerful being in
the world.

— Emmet Fox

≈ Easy Does It... ≈

Since there are opposites to all things, I will choose the easy instead of the difficult way.

I can choose relaxation or stress, detachment or control, acceptance or dominance, freedom or attachment, peace or strife, joy or sorrow, and bliss or misery.

I will remember that when the hard way presents itself, it is only one side of things and doesn't deserve my attention.

When my mind is at rest and I am empty and receptive, the easy and beautiful unfolding takes place. This is known as recovering the easy way.

— Jim McGregor

Simplicity is an exact medium between too little and too much.

— Sir Joshua Reynolds

Learn to say no...

The most important thing you can do for yourself in a crisis situation is to learn to manage your time. You have to put yourself first on your agenda. The best way to do that is to learn to say no. You can no longer afford to live within the perception that you're going to miss out on something potentially life-changing if you're not there, whether the event is a new movie that everyone's going to see, or a family wedding, or a business meeting.

— Caroline Myss

God, give us grace to accept with
SERENITY
the things that cannot be changed,
COURAGE
to change the things which should be changed, and the
WISDOM
to distinguish the one from the other.

 Reinhold Niebuhr

As human beings, we're not perfect,
and we're not supposed to be.
But that's not always an easy thing for us to realize.
The best we can do is to do the best we can,
give it our all, and always give thanks.
We don't make it alone in this world.
We're lucky that there are people
placed in our path to guide us,
protect us, and touch our lives
so that we can get through it all...
one day at a time.

— Julia Escobar

We are all travellers in the
wilderness of this world,
and the best that we find in our travels
is an honest friend.

— Robert Louis Stevenson

Community

Recovery leads to a sense of community.

Recovering people have a common bond.

Recovering people treat each other as longtime friends.

Recovering people become simple and honest with themselves.

Recovering people have a sense of their mortality.

Recovering people consider their fellows as their family.

Recovering people allow their fellows to live and die
with respect.

Recovering people are special... but they are ordinary.

 Jim McGregor

We are here
to help
each other.

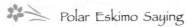 Polar Eskimo Saying

The Road to Recovery

The road to recovery
is sometimes slow.
But may your path
be made easier
just by knowing
that God is watching over you
while friends and family
stand beside you,
caring and concerned.
Together,
they all join forces for you,
praying that your recovery
will be complete and full
and soon.

Linda E. Knight

"One Day at a Time"

Our lives are made up of a million moments, spent in a million different ways. Some are spent searching for love, peace, and harmony. Others are spent surviving day to day. But there is no greater moment than when we find that life — with all its joys and sorrows — is meant to be lived one day at a time.

It's in this knowledge that we discover the most wonderful truth of all. Whether we live in a forty-room mansion surrounded by servants and wealth, or find it a struggle to manage the rent month to month, we have it within our power to be fully satisfied and live a life with true meaning.

One day at a time — we have that ability, through cherishing each moment and rejoicing in each dream. We can experience each day anew, and with this fresh start we have what it takes to make all of our dreams come true. Each day is new, and living one day at a time enables us to truly enjoy life and live it to the fullest.

— Regina Hill

ACKNOWLEDGMENTS

We gratefully acknowledge the permission granted by the following authors, publishers, and authors' representatives to reprint poems or excerpts from their publications.

Foundation for *A Course in Miracles* for "Every situation..." from A COURSE IN MIRACLES. Copyright © 1975, 1992, 1999 by the Foundation for *A Course in Miracles*. All rights reserved. Reprinted by permission of the Foundation for *A Course in Miracles*, 1275 Tennanah Lake Road, Roscoe, NY 12776-5905.

Harmony Books, a division of Random House, Inc., for "Accept what comes..." and "The use of love..." from JOURNEY INTO HEALING by Deepak Chopra, M.D. Copyright © 1994 by Deepak Chopra, M.D. All rights reserved. Reprinted by permission.

Crown Publishers, Inc., a division of Random House, Inc., for "Learn to say no..." from WHY PEOPLE DON'T HEAL AND HOW THEY CAN by Caroline Myss, Ph.D. Copyright © 1997 by Caroline Myss. And for "Recovery from any illness..." from FOOD FOR RECOVERY by Joseph D. Beasley, M.D. and Susan Knightly. Copyright © 1994 by Joseph D. Beasley, M.D. and Susan Knightly. All rights reserved. Reprinted by permission.

HarperCollins Publishers, Inc. for "Sometimes when we pray..." and "Find places of healing..." from JOURNEY TO THE HEART: DAILY MEDITATIONS ON THE PATH TO FREEING YOUR SOUL by Melody Beattie. Copyright © 1996 by Melody Beattie. And for "Life is difficult..." and "When someone you love..." from HOW TO LIVE BETWEEN OFFICE VISITS by Bernie S. Siegel, M.D. Copyright © 1993 by Bernie S. Siegel. All rights reserved. Reprinted by permission.

Veronica A. Shoffstall for "After a While." Copyright © 1971 by Veronica A. Shoffstall. All rights reserved. Reprinted by permission.

PrimaDonna Entertainment Corp. for "You'll Get Through This... One Day at a Time" and "Remember: the will is mighty..." by Donna Fargo. Copyright © 2000 by PrimaDonna Entertainment Corp. All rights reserved. Reprinted by permission.

Essence Communications, Inc. for "We bring about new beginnings..." from IN THE SPIRIT: THE INSPIRATIONAL WRITINGS OF SUSAN L. TAYLOR, published by Amistad. Copyright © 1993 by Essence Communications, Inc. All rights reserved. Reprinted by permission.

Jeremy P. Tarcher, a division of Penguin Putnam, Inc., for "An essential part..." by Shakti Gawain, "Healing is... peeling away the barriers..." by Joan Borysenko, "Healing is... natural..." by Rachel Naomi Remen, and "Healing... is releasing..." by Gerald Jampolsky from HEALERS ON HEALING edited by Benjamin Shield and Richard Carlson. Copyright © 1989 by Benjamin Shield and Richard Carlson. And for "In every event..." from BLESSINGS: PRAYERS AND DECLARATIONS FOR A HEARTFUL LIFE by Julia Cameron. Copyright © 1998 by Julia Cameron. All rights reserved. Reprinted by permission.

Putnam Berkley, a division of Penguin Putnam, Inc., for "Put knowledge, faith, and ideals..." from IN SEARCH OF HEALING by William A. McGarey, M.D. Copyright © 1996 by William A. McGarey, M.D. All rights reserved. Reprinted by permission.

Hay House, Inc. for "We create our reality..." and "Trust the Process of Life" from MEDITATIONS TO HEAL YOUR LIFE by Louise L. Hay. Copyright © 1994 by Louise L. Hay. And for "If you seek peace..." from THE POWER OF THE MIND TO HEAL by Joan Borysenko, Ph.D. and Miroslav Borysenko, Ph.D. Copyright © 1994 by Joan Borysenko and Miroslav Borysenko. All rights reserved. Reprinted by permission of Hay House, Inc., Carlsbad, CA.

Donna Newman for "Recovery is... about learning...." Copyright © 2000 by Donna Newman. All rights reserved. Reprinted by permission.

Josie Willis for "Recovery is... sometimes a long road...." Copyright © 2000 by Josie Willis. All rights reserved. Reprinted by permission.

Tim Connor for "My Wounded Child." Copyright © 2000 by Tim Connor. All rights reserved. Reprinted by permission.

Wendy Apgar for "Life." Copyright © 1997 by Wendy Apgar. All rights reserved. Reprinted by permission.

Barbara J. Hall for "Survivors Always Find a Way to Make the Best of Life." Copyright © 2000 by Barbara J. Hall. All rights reserved. Reprinted by permission.

Doubleday, a division of Random House, Inc., for "To have a hold on us..." from NOTES ON HOW TO LIVE IN THE WORLD... AND STILL BE HAPPY by Hugh Prather. Copyright © 1986 by Hugh Prather. All rights reserved. Reprinted by permission.

Humanics Publishing Group for "Since there are opposites..." and "Recovery leads..." from THE TAO OF RECOVERY: A QUIET PATH TO WHOLENESS by Jim McGregor. Copyright © 1992 by Humanics Limited. All rights reserved. Reprinted by permission.

A careful effort has been made to trace the ownership of poems used in this anthology in order to obtain permission to reprint copyrighted materials and give proper credit to the copyright owners. If any error or omission has occurred, it is completely inadvertent, and we would like to make corrections in future editions provided that written notification is made to the publisher:

SPS STUDIOS, INC., P.O. Box 4549, Boulder, Colorado 80306.